www.powerofyet.com

A review on Amazon will be
highly appreciated.
Thanks!

My Journey To More Happiness

Please read this

Do you sometimes feel rushed and forget to feel the happiness in your life? That's how I felt after having my son. Life got so unbelievably busy.

I invested time learning more about how I could increase happiness. I read papers and books and participated in online courses. I found that happiness is something that can actually be studied. It's relatively easy. You ask people how happy they are on a scale from 1 to 5, do an intervention, and ask again. Voila. Guessing is over. Researchers do these experiments all the time. Obviously, their experiments are more sophisticated, but the main point is:

We know what increases happiness.

We also know that a good paying job, a nice car, plastic surgery, and other things like these are not making us happy long term. **This workbook is focused on being active and trying the things we know that have been proven to boost happiness.** I won't explain why the things you think will make you happy actually don't. But I won't leave you hanging. There are two resources I encourage you to check out if you want to understand the science behind these tasks.

- Participate in the FREE online course from Laurie Santos, "**The Science of Well-Being**", on Coursera. Laurie Santos has an amazing course collecting all the different experiments and studies done that will ultimately answer the questions on how to be happier. I highly recommend you take the time to do the 10-week online course. It's an eye-opening experience. What could be better than spending your time learning about how to be happier?

- Read or listen to the book, ***Atomic Habits* by James Clear**. Why? Knowing what to do is often not enough. The task you are going to do in this workbook seems easy, but the only way of sticking with it is to develop a habit. James Clear does an awesome job in explaining how that can be achieved.

Many self-help books sound logical and inspirational, but when it comes to implementing, they often failed me.

I wanted to focus on **actionable things that are scientifically proven to increase happiness.**

I created my very own happiness workbook that I'm sharing with you now. The biggest misconception that people have is knowing is half the battle. It is NOT. Not even close. This workbook will help you to stay consistent with your happiness practice. You can **start immediately** and don't need to read through all the pages and self-help books. Doing is more important than reading.

Putting the methods into practice and tracking your results will lead to an increase of happiness. But don't get me wrong. **It is not easy.** Don't get discouraged when you struggle sticking with a method or forget to track your data. Just revisit this workbook and start fresh. Once you feel the happiness boost you receive from doing these methods, it will get easier.

Good luck on your journey. I wish you bravery, endurance, and a lot of happiness!

Power Of Yet - Team

How to use this workbook

This workbook offers you **six scientifically proven methods** to boost your happiness:

Sleep	Gratitude	Exercise
Meditation	Kindness	Connection

- Focus on one or **two methods per week** to find the ones that work best for you and your life.
- Evaluate the method at the end of the happiness workbook.

Voila! You just found ways that work to improve your happiness. Use the rest of the tracking sheets to stick with your favorite methods.

Congratulations!

This week I will focus on:

Circle one or two:

Sleep	Gratitude	Exercise
Meditation	Kindness	Connection

Sleep

Mark each day of the week you got more than 7 hours of sleep.

Sun. Mon. Tues. Wed. Thurs. Fri. Sat.

Acts of Kindness

Choose one day of the week to do five kind things. Research shows highest amount of happiness happens when you do five kind things on one day instead of one kind thing a day.

1.
2.
3.
4.
5.

Bonus

Exercise

Mark each day of the week when you exercised more than 30 minutes.

Sun. Mon. Tues. Wed. Thurs. Fri. Sat.

Type of exercise: ____________________

Goal: How many days of the week: ____________________

Week: ____________

Meditation

Mark each day of the week you meditated.

Sun. Mon. Tues. Wed. Thurs. Fri. Sat.

Individual goal (lengths of meditation): ____________

Gratitude journal

Two small things:

____

____

____

____

Two bigger things:

____

____

____

____

Social Connection

Mark each day of the week you talked or smiled at a stranger or talked to a friend.

Sun. Mon. Tues. Wed. Thurs. Fri. Sat.

This week I feel:

This week I will focus on:

Circle one or two:

Sleep	Gratitude	Exercise
Meditation	Kindness	Connection

Sleep

Mark each day of the week you got more than 7 hours of sleep.

Sun Mon Tues Wed Thurs Fri Sat

Acts of Kindness

Choose one day of the week to do five kind things. Research shows highest amount of happiness happens when you do five kind things on one day instead of one kind thing a day.

1. ____________________
2. ____________________
3. ____________________
4. ____________________
5. ____________________

Bonus ____________________

Exercise

Mark each day of the week when you exercised more than 30 minutes.

Sun Mon Tues Wed Thurs Fri Sat

Type of exercise: ____________________

Goal: How many days of the week: ____________________

Week:_____________

Meditation

Mark each day of the week you meditated.

Sun. Mon. Tues. Wed. Thurs. Fri. Sat.

Individual goal (lengths of meditation): ______________

Gratitude journal

Two small things:

____

____

____

____

Two bigger things:

____

____

____

____

Social Connection

Mark each day of the week you talked or smiled at a stranger or talked to a friend.

Sun. Mon. Tues. Wed. Thurs. Fri. Sat.

This week I feel:

This week I will focus on:

Circle one or two:

Sleep	Gratitude	Exercise
Meditation	Kindness	Connection

Sleep

Mark each day of the week you got more than 7 hours of sleep.

Sun. Mon. Tues. Wed. Thurs. Fri. Sat.

Acts of Kindness

Choose one day of the week to do five kind things. Research shows highest amount of happiness happens when you do five kind things on one day instead of one kind thing a day.

1. ______
2. ______
3. ______
4. ______
5. ______

Bonus ______

Exercise

Mark each day of the week when you exercised more than 30 minutes.

Sun. Mon. Tues. Wed. Thurs. Fri. Sat.

Type of exercise: ______

Goal: How many days of the week: ______

Week: ____________

Meditation

Mark each day of the week you meditated.

Sun. Mon. Tues. Wed. Thurs. Fri. Sat.

Individual goal (lengths of meditation): ____________

Gratitude journal

Two small things:

____
____
____
____

Two bigger things:

____
____
____
____

Social Connection

Mark each day of the week you talked or smiled at a stranger or talked to a friend.

Sun. Mon. Tues. Wed. Thurs. Fri. Sat.

This week I feel:

This week I will focus on:

Circle one or two:

Sleep	Gratitude	Exercise
Meditation	Kindness	Connection

Sleep

Mark each day of the week you got more than 7 hours of sleep.

Sun. Mon. Tues. Wed. Thurs. Fri. Sat.

Acts of Kindness

Choose one day of the week to do five kind things. Research shows highest amount of happiness happens when you do five kind things on one day instead of one kind thing a day.

1. ___
2. ___
3. ___
4. ___
5. ___

Bonus ___

Exercise

Mark each day of the week when you exercised more than 30 minutes.

Sun. Mon. Tues. Wed. Thurs. Fri. Sat.

Type of exercise: ___

Goal: How many days of the week: ___

Week:____________

Meditation

Mark each day of the week you meditated.

Sun. Mon. Tues. Wed. Thurs. Fri. Sat.

Individual goal (lengths of meditation): ____________

Gratitude journal

Two small things:

____

____

____

____

Two bigger things:

____

____

____

____

Social Connection

Mark each day of the week you talked or smiled at a stranger or talked to a friend.

Sun. Mon. Tues. Wed. Thurs. Fri. Sat.

This week I feel:

This week I will focus on:

Circle one or two:

Sleep	Gratitude	Exercise
Meditation	Kindness	Connection

Sleep

Mark each day of the week you got more than 7 hours of sleep.

Sun. Mon. Tues. Wed. Thurs. Fri. Sat.

Acts of Kindness

Choose one day of the week to do five kind things. Research shows highest amount of happiness happens when you do five kind things on one day instead of one kind thing a day.

1.
2.
3.
4.
5.

Bonus

Exercise

Mark each day of the week when you exercised more than 30 minutes.

Sun. Mon. Tues. Wed. Thurs. Fri. Sat.

Type of exercise: ____________________

Goal: How many days of the week: ____________________

Week: ____________

Meditation

Mark each day of the week you meditated.

Sun. Mon. Tues. Wed. Thurs. Fri. Sat.

Individual goal (lengths of meditation): ____________

Gratitude journal

Two small things:

____

____

____

____

Two bigger things:

____

____

____

____

Social Connection

Mark each day of the week you talked or smiled at a stranger or talked to a friend.

Sun. Mon. Tues. Wed. Thurs. Fri. Sat.

This week I feel:

This week I will focus on:

Circle one or two:

Sleep	Gratitude	Exercise
Meditation	Kindness	Connection

Sleep

Mark each day of the week you got more than 7 hours of sleep.

Sun. Mon. Tues. Wed. Thurs. Fri. Sat.

Acts of Kindness

Choose one day of the week to do five kind things. Research shows highest amount of happiness happens when you do five kind things on one day instead of one kind thing a day.

1. ____________________
2. ____________________
3. ____________________
4. ____________________
5. ____________________

Bonus ____________________

Exercise

Mark each day of the week when you exercised more than 30 minutes.

Sun. Mon. Tues. Wed. Thurs. Fri. Sat.

Type of exercise: ____________________

Goal: How many days of the week: ____________________

Week: ____________

Meditation

Mark each day of the week you meditated.

Sun. Mon. Tues. Wed. Thurs. Fri. Sat.

Individual goal (lengths of meditation): ____________

Gratitude journal

Two small things:

____

____

____

____

Two bigger things:

____

____

____

____

Social Connection

Mark each day of the week you talked or smiled at a stranger or talked to a friend.

Sun. Mon. Tues. Wed. Thurs. Fri. Sat.

This week I feel:

This week I will focus on:

Circle one or two:

Sleep	Gratitude	Exercise
Meditation	Kindness	Connection

Sleep

Mark each day of the week you got more than 7 hours of sleep.

Sun. Mon. Tues. Wed. Thurs. Fri. Sat.

Acts of Kindness

Choose one day of the week to do five kind things. Research shows highest amount of happiness happens when you do five kind things on one day instead of one kind thing a day.

1. ____________________
2. ____________________
3. ____________________
4. ____________________
5. ____________________

Bonus ____________________

Exercise

Mark each day of the week when you exercised more than 30 minutes.

Sun. Mon. Tues. Wed. Thurs. Fri. Sat.

Type of exercise: ____________________

Goal: How many days of the week: ____________________

Week: ___________

Meditation

Mark each day of the week you meditated.

Sun. Mon. Tues. Wed. Thurs. Fri. Sat.

Individual goal (lengths of meditation): ___________

Gratitude journal

Two small things:

Two bigger things:

Social Connection

Mark each day of the week you talked or smiled at a stranger or talked to a friend.

Sun. Mon. Tues. Wed. Thurs. Fri. Sat.

This week I feel:

This week I will focus on:

Circle one or two:

Sleep	Gratitude	Exercise
Meditation	Kindness	Connection

Sleep

Mark each day of the week you got more than 7 hours of sleep.

Sun. Mon. Tues. Wed. Thurs. Fri. Sat.

Acts of Kindness

Choose one day of the week to do five kind things. Research shows highest amount of happiness happens when you do five kind things on one day instead of one kind thing a day.

1. ______________________
2. ______________________
3. ______________________
4. ______________________
5. ______________________

Bonus ______________________

Exercise

Mark each day of the week when you exercised more than 30 minutes.

Sun. Mon. Tues. Wed. Thurs. Fri. Sat.

Type of exercise: ______________________

Goal: How many days of the week: ______________________

Week:____________

Meditation

Mark each day of the week you meditated.

Sun Mon. Tues Wed Thurs Fri Sat

Individual goal (lengths of meditation): ____________

Gratitude journal

Two small things:

____

____

____

____

Two bigger things:

____

____

____

____

Social Connection

Mark each day of the week you talked or smiled at a stranger or talked to a friend.

Sun Mon. Tues. Wed Thurs Fri Sat

This week I feel:

This week I will focus on:

Circle one or two:

Sleep	Gratitude	Exercise
Meditation	Kindness	Connection

Sleep

Mark each day of the week you got more than 7 hours of sleep.

Sun Mon Tues Wed Thurs Fri Sat

Acts of Kindness

Choose one day of the week to do five kind things. Research shows highest amount of happiness happens when you do five kind things on one day instead of one kind thing a day.

1. ____________________
2. ____________________
3. ____________________
4. ____________________
5. ____________________

Bonus ____________________

Exercise

Mark each day of the week when you exercised more than 30 minutes.

Sun Mon Tues Wed Thurs Fri Sat

Type of exercise: ____________________

Goal: How many days of the week: ____________________

Week: ____________

Meditation

Mark each day of the week you meditated.

Sun. Mon. Tues. Wed. Thurs. Fri. Sat.

Individual goal (lengths of meditation): ____________

Gratitude journal

Two small things:

Two bigger things:

Social Connection

Mark each day of the week you talked or smiled at a stranger or talked to a friend.

Sun. Mon. Tues. Wed. Thurs. Fri. Sat.

This week I feel:

This week I will focus on:

Circle one or two:

Sleep	Gratitude	Exercise
Meditation	Kindness	Connection

Sleep

Mark each day of the week you got more than 7 hours of sleep.

Sun. Mon. Tues. Wed. Thurs. Fri. Sat.

Acts of Kindness

Choose one day of the week to do five kind things. Research shows highest amount of happiness happens when you do five kind things on one day instead of one kind thing a day.

1. ______
2. ______
3. ______
4. ______
5. ______

Bonus ______

Exercise

Mark each day of the week when you exercised more than 30 minutes.

Sun. Mon. Tues. Wed. Thurs. Fri. Sat.

Type of exercise: ______

Goal: How many days of the week: ______

Week: ____________

Meditation

Mark each day of the week you meditated.

Sun. Mon. Tues. Wed. Thurs. Fri. Sat.

Individual goal (lengths of meditation): ____________

Gratitude journal

Two small things:

____

____

____

____

Two bigger things:

____

____

____

____

Social Connection

Mark each day of the week you talked or smiled at a stranger or talked to a friend.

Sun. Mon. Tues. Wed. Thurs. Fri. Sat.

This week I feel:

This week I will focus on:

Circle one or two:

Sleep	Gratitude	Exercise
Meditation	Kindness	Connection

Sleep

Mark each day of the week you got more than 7 hours of sleep.

Sun. Mon. Tues. Wed. Thurs. Fri. Sat.

Acts of Kindness

Choose one day of the week to do five kind things. Research shows highest amount of happiness happens when you do five kind things on one day instead of one kind thing a day.

1. ______
2. ______
3. ______
4. ______
5. ______

Bonus ______

Exercise

Mark each day of the week when you exercised more than 30 minutes.

Sun. Mon. Tues. Wed. Thurs. Fri. Sat.

Type of exercise: ______

Goal: How many days of the week: ______

Week: ____________

Meditation

Mark each day of the week you meditated.

Sun. | Mon. | Tues. | Wed. | Thurs. | Fri. | Sat.

Individual goal (lengths of meditation): ____________

Gratitude journal

Two small things:

____

____

____

____

Two bigger things:

____

____

____

____

Social Connection

Mark each day of the week you talked or smiled at a stranger or talked to a friend.

Sun. | Mon. | Tues. | Wed. | Thurs. | Fri. | Sat.

This week I feel:

This week I will focus on:

Circle one or two:

Sleep	Gratitude	Exercise
Meditation	Kindness	Connection

Sleep

Mark each day of the week you got more than 7 hours of sleep.

Sun. Mon. Tues. Wed. Thurs. Fri. Sat.

Acts of Kindness

Choose one day of the week to do five kind things. Research shows highest amount of happiness happens when you do five kind things on one day instead of one kind thing a day.

1. ____________________
2. ____________________
3. ____________________
4. ____________________
5. ____________________

Bonus ____________________

Exercise

Mark each day of the week when you exercised more than 30 minutes.

Sun. Mon. Tues. Wed. Thurs. Fri. Sat.

Type of exercise: ____________________

Goal: How many days of the week: ____________________

Week:___________

Meditation

Mark each day of the week you meditated.

Sun. Mon. Tues. Wed. Thurs. Fri. Sat.

Individual goal (lengths of meditation): ___________

Gratitude journal

Two small things:

____

____

____

____

Two bigger things:

____

____

____

____

Social Connection

Mark each day of the week you talked or smiled at a stranger or talked to a friend.

Sun. Mon. Tues. Wed. Thurs. Fri. Sat.

This week I feel:

This week I will focus on:

Circle one or two:

Sleep	Gratitude	Exercise
Meditation	Kindness	Connection

Sleep

Mark each day of the week you got more than 7 hours of sleep.

Sun. Mon. Tues. Wed. Thurs. Fri. Sat.

Acts of Kindness

Choose one day of the week to do five kind things. Research shows highest amount of happiness happens when you do five kind things on one day instead of one kind thing a day.

1. __________
2. __________
3. __________
4. __________
5. __________

Bonus __________

Exercise

Mark each day of the week when you exercised more than 30 minutes.

Sun. Mon. Tues. Wed. Thurs. Fri. Sat.

Type of exercise: __________

Goal: How many days of the week: __________

Week:____________

Meditation

Mark each day of the week you meditated.

Sun. Mon. Tues. Wed. Thurs. Fri. Sat.

Individual goal (lengths of meditation): __________

Gratitude journal

Two small things:

Two bigger things:

Social Connection

Mark each day of the week you talked or smiled at a stranger or talked to a friend.

Sun. Mon. Tues. Wed. Thurs. Fri. Sat.

This week I feel:

This week I will focus on:

Circle one or two:

Sleep	Gratitude	Exercise
Meditation	Kindness	Connection

Sleep

Mark each day of the week you got more than 7 hours of sleep.

Sun. Mon. Tues. Wed. Thurs. Fri. Sat.

Acts of Kindness

Choose one day of the week to do five kind things. Research shows highest amount of happiness happens when you do five kind things on one day instead of one kind thing a day.

1. ______
2. ______
3. ______
4. ______
5. ______

Bonus ______

Exercise

Mark each day of the week when you exercised more than 30 minutes.

Sun. Mon. Tues. Wed. Thurs. Fri. Sat.

Type of exercise: ______

Goal: How many days of the week: ______

Week:___________

Meditation

Mark each day of the week you meditated.

Sun. Mon. Tues. Wed. Thurs. Fri. Sat.

Individual goal (lengths of meditation): ___________

Gratitude journal

Two small things:

Two bigger things:

Social Connection

Mark each day of the week you talked or smiled at a stranger or talked to a friend.

Sun. Mon. Tues. Wed. Thurs. Fri. Sat.

This week I feel:

This week I will focus on:

Circle one or two:

Sleep	Gratitude	Exercise
Meditation	Kindness	Connection

Sleep

Mark each day of the week you got more than 7 hours of sleep.

Sun. Mon. Tues. Wed. Thurs. Fri. Sat.

Acts of Kindness

Choose one day of the week to do five kind things. Research shows highest amount of happiness happens when you do five kind things on one day instead of one kind thing a day.

1. ____________________
2. ____________________
3. ____________________
4. ____________________
5. ____________________

Bonus ____________________

Exercise

Mark each day of the week when you exercised more than 30 minutes.

Sun. Mon. Tues. Wed. Thurs. Fri. Sat.

Type of exercise: ________________

Goal: How many days of the week: ________

Week: ____________

Meditation

Mark each day of the week you meditated.

Sun. Mon. Tues. Wed. Thurs. Fri. Sat.

Individual goal (lengths of meditation): ____________

Gratitude journal

Two small things:

Two bigger things:

Social Connection

Mark each day of the week you talked or smiled at a stranger or talked to a friend.

Sun. Mon. Tues. Wed. Thurs. Fri. Sat.

This week I feel:

This week I will focus on:

Circle one or two:

Sleep	Gratitude	Exercise
Meditation	Kindness	Connection

Sleep

Mark each day of the week you got more than 7 hours of sleep.

Sun. Mon. Tues. Wed. Thurs. Fri. Sat.

Acts of Kindness

Choose one day of the week to do five kind things. Research shows highest amount of happiness happens when you do five kind things on one day instead of one kind thing a day.

1. __________
2. __________
3. __________
4. __________
5. __________

Bonus __________

Exercise

Mark each day of the week when you exercised more than 30 minutes.

Sun. Mon. Tues. Wed. Thurs. Fri. Sat.

Type of exercise: __________

Goal: How many days of the week: __________

Week: ____________

Meditation

Mark each day of the week you meditated.

Sun. Mon. Tues. Wed. Thurs. Fri. Sat.

Individual goal (lengths of meditation): __________

Gratitude journal

Two small things:

____

____

____

____

Two bigger things:

____

____

____

____

Social Connection

Mark each day of the week you talked or smiled at a stranger or talked to a friend.

Sun. Mon. Tues. Wed. Thurs. Fri. Sat.

This week I feel:

This week I will focus on:

Circle one or two:

Sleep	Gratitude	Exercise
Meditation	Kindness	Connection

Sleep

Mark each day of the week you got more than 7 hours of sleep.

Sun. Mon. Tues. Wed. Thurs. Fri. Sat.

Acts of Kindness

Choose one day of the week to do five kind things. Research shows highest amount of happiness happens when you do five kind things on one day instead of one kind thing a day.

1. ______
2. ______
3. ______
4. ______
5. ______

Bonus ______

Exercise

Mark each day of the week when you exercised more than 30 minutes.

Sun. Mon. Tues. Wed. Thurs. Fri. Sat.

Type of exercise: ______

Goal: How many days of the week: ______

Week: ____________

Meditation

Mark each day of the week you meditated.

Sun. Mon. Tues. Wed. Thurs. Fri. Sat.

Individual goal (lengths of meditation): ____________

Gratitude journal

Two small things:

____

____

____

____

Two bigger things:

____

____

____

____

Social Connection

Mark each day of the week you talked or smiled at a stranger or talked to a friend.

Sun. Mon. Tues. Wed. Thurs. Fri. Sat.

This week I feel:

This week I will focus on:

Circle one or two:

Sleep	Gratitude	Exercise
Meditation	Kindness	Connection

Sleep

Mark each day of the week you got more than 7 hours of sleep.

Sun. Mon. Tues. Wed. Thurs. Fri. Sat.

Acts of Kindness

Choose one day of the week to do five kind things. Research shows highest amount of happiness happens when you do five kind things on one day instead of one kind thing a day.

1. ______
2. ______
3. ______
4. ______
5. ______

Bonus ______

Exercise

Mark each day of the week when you exercised more than 30 minutes.

Sun. Mon. Tues. Wed. Thurs. Fri. Sat.

Type of exercise: ______

Goal: How many days of the week: ______

Week: ____________

Meditation

Mark each day of the week you meditated.

Sun. Mon. Tues. Wed. Thurs. Fri. Sat.

Individual goal (lengths of meditation): ____________

Gratitude journal

Two small things:

Two bigger things:

Social Connection

Mark each day of the week you talked or smiled at a stranger or talked to a friend.

Sun. Mon. Tues. Wed. Thurs. Fri. Sat.

This week I feel:

This week I will focus on:

Circle one or two:

Sleep	Gratitude	Exercise
Meditation	Kindness	Connection

Sleep

Mark each day of the week you got more than 7 hours of sleep.

Sun. Mon. Tues. Wed. Thurs. Fri. Sat.

Acts of Kindness

Choose one day of the week to do five kind things. Research shows highest amount of happiness happens when you do five kind things on one day instead of one kind thing a day.

1. ______
2. ______
3. ______
4. ______
5. ______

Bonus ______

Exercise

Mark each day of the week when you exercised more than 30 minutes.

Sun. Mon. Tues. Wed. Thurs. Fri. Sat.

Type of exercise: ______

Goal: How many days of the week: ______

Week:_____________

Meditation

Mark each day of the week you meditated.

Sun. Mon. Tues. Wed. Thurs. Fri. Sat.

Individual goal (lengths of meditation): ____________

Gratitude journal

Two small things:

Two bigger things:

Social Connection

Mark each day of the week you talked or smiled at a stranger or talked to a friend.

Sun. Mon. Tues. Wed. Thurs. Fri. Sat.

This week I feel:

This week I will focus on:

Circle one or two:

Sleep	Gratitude	Exercise
Meditation	Kindness	Connection

Sleep

Mark each day of the week you got more than 7 hours of sleep.

Sun. Mon. Tues. Wed. Thurs. Fri. Sat.

Acts of Kindness

Choose one day of the week to do five kind things. Research shows highest amount of happiness happens when you do five kind things on one day instead of one kind thing a day.

1. ______
2. ______
3. ______
4. ______
5. ______

Bonus ______

Exercise

Mark each day of the week when you exercised more than 30 minutes.

Sun. Mon. Tues. Wed. Thurs. Fri. Sat.

Type of exercise: ______

Goal: How many days of the week: ______

Week: ____________

Meditation

Mark each day of the week you meditated.

Sun. Mon. Tues. Wed. Thurs. Fri. Sat.

Individual goal (lengths of meditation): ____________

Gratitude journal

Two small things:

Two bigger things:

Social Connection

Mark each day of the week you talked or smiled at a stranger or talked to a friend.

Sun. Mon. Tues. Wed. Thurs. Fri. Sat.

This week I feel:

This week I will focus on:

Circle one or two:

Sleep	Gratitude	Exercise
Meditation	Kindness	Connection

Sleep

Mark each day of the week you got more than 7 hours of sleep.

Sun. Mon. Tues. Wed. Thurs. Fri. Sat.

Acts of Kindness

Choose one day of the week to do five kind things. Research shows highest amount of happiness happens when you do five kind things on one day instead of one kind thing a day.

1. ____________________
2. ____________________
3. ____________________
4. ____________________
5. ____________________

Bonus ____________________

Exercise

Mark each day of the week when you exercised more than 30 minutes.

Sun. Mon. Tues. Wed. Thurs. Fri. Sat.

Type of exercise: ____________________

Goal: How many days of the week: ____________________

Week: ____________

Meditation

Mark each day of the week you meditated.

Sun. Mon. Tues. Wed. Thurs. Fri. Sat.

Individual goal (lengths of meditation): ____________

Gratitude journal

Two small things:

____

____

____

____

Two bigger things:

____

____

____

____

Social Connection

Mark each day of the week you talked or smiled at a stranger or talked to a friend.

Sun. Mon. Tues. Wed. Thurs. Fri. Sat.

This week I feel:

This week I will focus on:

Circle one or two:

Sleep	Gratitude	Exercise
Meditation	Kindness	Connection

Sleep

Mark each day of the week you got more than 7 hours of sleep.

Sun. Mon. Tues. Wed. Thurs. Fri. Sat.

Acts of Kindness

Choose one day of the week to do five kind things. Research shows highest amount of happiness happens when you do five kind things on one day instead of one kind thing a day.

1. __________
2. __________
3. __________
4. __________
5. __________

Bonus __________

Exercise

Mark each day of the week when you exercised more than 30 minutes.

Sun. Mon. Tues. Wed. Thurs. Fri. Sat.

Type of exercise: __________

Goal: How many days of the week: __________

Week: ____________

Meditation

Mark each day of the week you meditated.

Sun. Mon. Tues. Wed. Thurs. Fri. Sat.

Individual goal (lengths of meditation): ____________

Gratitude journal

Two small things:

Two bigger things:

Social Connection

Mark each day of the week you talked or smiled at a stranger or talked to a friend.

Sun. Mon. Tues. Wed. Thurs. Fri. Sat.

This week I feel:

This week I will focus on:

Circle one or two:

Sleep	Gratitude	Exercise
Meditation	Kindness	Connection

Sleep

Mark each day of the week you got more than 7 hours of sleep.

Sun. Mon. Tues. Wed. Thurs. Fri. Sat.

Acts of Kindness

Choose one day of the week to do five kind things. Research shows highest amount of happiness happens when you do five kind things on one day instead of one kind thing a day.

1. ____________________
2. ____________________
3. ____________________
4. ____________________
5. ____________________

Bonus ____________________

Exercise

Mark each day of the week when you exercised more than 30 minutes.

Sun. Mon. Tues. Wed. Thurs. Fri. Sat.

Type of exercise: ____________________

Goal: How many days of the week: ____________________

Week: ____________

Meditation

Mark each day of the week you meditated.

Sun. Mon. Tues. Wed. Thurs. Fri. Sat.

Individual goal (lengths of meditation): ____________

Gratitude journal

Two small things:

____

____

____

____

Two bigger things:

____

____

____

____

Social Connection

Mark each day of the week you talked or smiled at a stranger or talked to a friend.

Sun. Mon. Tues. Wed. Thurs. Fri. Sat.

This week I feel:

This week I will focus on:

Circle one or two:

Sleep	Gratitude	Exercise
Meditation	Kindness	Connection

Sleep

Mark each day of the week you got more than 7 hours of sleep.

Sun. Mon. Tues. Wed. Thurs. Fri. Sat.

Acts of Kindness

Choose one day of the week to do five kind things. Research shows highest amount of happiness happens when you do five kind things on one day instead of one kind thing a day.

1. ______
2. ______
3. ______
4. ______
5. ______

Bonus ______

Exercise

Mark each day of the week when you exercised more than 30 minutes.

Sun. Mon. Tues. Wed. Thurs. Fri. Sat.

Type of exercise: ______

Goal: How many days of the week: ______

Week: ___________

Meditation

Mark each day of the week you meditated.

Sun. Mon. Tues. Wed. Thurs. Fri. Sat.

Individual goal (lengths of meditation): ___________

Gratitude journal

Two small things:

Two bigger things:

Social Connection

Mark each day of the week you talked or smiled at a stranger or talked to a friend.

Sun. Mon. Tues. Wed. Thurs. Fri. Sat.

This week I feel:

This week I will focus on:

Circle one or two:

Sleep	Gratitude	Exercise
Meditation	Kindness	Connection

Sleep

Mark each day of the week you got more than 7 hours of sleep.

Sun. Mon. Tues. Wed. Thurs. Fri. Sat.

Acts of Kindness

Choose one day of the week to do five kind things. Research shows highest amount of happiness happens when you do five kind things on one day instead of one kind thing a day.

1. ______
2. ______
3. ______
4. ______
5. ______

Bonus ______

Exercise

Mark each day of the week when you exercised more than 30 minutes.

Sun. Mon. Tues. Wed. Thurs. Fri. Sat.

Type of exercise: ______
Goal: How many days of the week: ______

Week: ____________

Meditation

Mark each day of the week you meditated.

Sun. Mon. Tues. Wed. Thurs. Fri. Sat.

Individual goal (lengths of meditation): __________

Gratitude journal

Two small things:

Two bigger things:

Social Connection

Mark each day of the week you talked or smiled at a stranger or talked to a friend.

Sun. Mon. Tues. Wed. Thurs. Fri. Sat.

This week I feel:

This week I will focus on:

Circle one or two:

Sleep	Gratitude	Exercise
Meditation	Kindness	Connection

Sleep

Mark each day of the week you got more than 7 hours of sleep.

Sun. Mon. Tues. Wed. Thurs. Fri. Sat.

Acts of Kindness

Choose one day of the week to do five kind things. Research shows highest amount of happiness happens when you do five kind things on one day instead of one kind thing a day.

1. ______
2. ______
3. ______
4. ______
5. ______

Bonus ______

Exercise

Mark each day of the week when you exercised more than 30 minutes.

Sun. Mon. Tues. Wed. Thurs. Fri. Sat.

Type of exercise: ______

Goal: How many days of the week: ______

Week: ____________

Meditation

Mark each day of the week you meditated.

Sun. Mon. Tues. Wed. Thurs. Fri. Sat.

Individual goal (lengths of meditation): ____________

Gratitude journal

Two small things:

Two bigger things:

Social Connection

Mark each day of the week you talked or smiled at a stranger or talked to a friend.

Sun. Mon. Tues. Wed. Thurs. Fri. Sat.

This week I feel:

This week I will focus on:

Circle one or two:

Sleep	Gratitude	Exercise
Meditation	Kindness	Connection

Sleep

Mark each day of the week you got more than 7 hours of sleep.

Sun. Mon. Tues. Wed. Thurs. Fri. Sat.

Acts of Kindness

Choose one day of the week to do five kind things. Research shows highest amount of happiness happens when you do five kind things on one day instead of one kind thing a day.

1. ______________________
2. ______________________
3. ______________________
4. ______________________
5. ______________________

Bonus ______________________

Exercise

Mark each day of the week when you exercised more than 30 minutes.

Sun. Mon. Tues. Wed. Thurs. Fri. Sat.

Type of exercise: ______________________

Goal: How many days of the week: ______________________

Week: ____________

Meditation

Mark each day of the week you meditated.

Sun. Mon. Tues. Wed. Thurs. Fri. Sat.

Individual goal (lengths of meditation): ____________

Gratitude journal

Two small things:

____

____

____

____

Two bigger things:

____

____

____

____

Social Connection

Mark each day of the week you talked or smiled at a stranger or talked to a friend.

Sun. Mon. Tues. Wed. Thurs. Fri. Sat.

This week I feel:

This week I will focus on:

Circle one or two:

Sleep	Gratitude	Exercise
Meditation	Kindness	Connection

Sleep

Mark each day of the week you got more than 7 hours of sleep.

Sun. Mon. Tues. Wed. Thurs. Fri. Sat.

Acts of Kindness

Choose one day of the week to do five kind things. Research shows highest amount of happiness happens when you do five kind things on one day instead of one kind thing a day.

1. ______
2. ______
3. ______
4. ______
5. ______

Bonus ______

Exercise

Mark each day of the week when you exercised more than 30 minutes.

Sun. Mon. Tues. Wed. Thurs. Fri. Sat.

Type of exercise: ______

Goal: How many days of the week: ______

Week: ____________

Meditation

Mark each day of the week you meditated.

Sun. Mon. Tues. Wed. Thurs. Fri. Sat.

Individual goal (lengths of meditation): ____________

Gratitude journal

Two small things:

Two bigger things:

Social Connection

Mark each day of the week you talked or smiled at a stranger or talked to a friend.

Sun. Mon. Tues. Wed. Thurs. Fri. Sat.

This week I feel:

This week I will focus on:

Circle one or two:

Sleep	Gratitude	Exercise
Meditation	Kindness	Connection

Sleep

Mark each day of the week you got more than 7 hours of sleep.

Sun. Mon. Tues. Wed. Thurs. Fri. Sat.

Acts of Kindness

Choose one day of the week to do five kind things. Research shows highest amount of happiness happens when you do five kind things on one day instead of one kind thing a day.

1. __________
2. __________
3. __________
4. __________
5. __________

Bonus __________

Exercise

Mark each day of the week when you exercised more than 30 minutes.

Sun. Mon. Tues. Wed. Thurs. Fri. Sat.

Type of exercise: __________

Goal: How many days of the week: __________

Week: ___ ______

Meditation

Mark each day of the week you meditated.

Sun. Mon. Tues. Wed. Thurs. Fri. Sat.

Individual goal (lengths of meditation): ____________

Gratitude journal

Two small things:

____

____

____

____

Two bigger things:

____

____

____

____

Social Connection

Mark each day of the week you talked or smiled at a stranger or talked to a friend

Sun. Mon. Tues. Wed. Thurs. Fri. Sat.

This week I feel:

This week I will focus on:

Circle one or two:

Sleep	Gratitude	Exercise
Meditation	Kindness	Connection

Sleep

Mark each day of the week you got more than 7 hours of sleep.

Sun. Mon. Tues. Wed. Thurs. Fri. Sat.

Acts of Kindness

Choose one day of the week to do five kind things. Research shows highest amount of happiness happens when you do five kind things on one day instead of one kind thing a day.

1. ______
2. ______
3. ______
4. ______
5. ______

Bonus ______

Exercise

Mark each day of the week when you exercised more than 30 minutes.

Sun. Mon. Tues. Wed. Thurs. Fri. Sat.

Type of exercise: ______
Goal: How many days of the week: ______

Week: ____________

Meditation

Mark each day of the week you meditated.

Sun. Mon. Tues. Wed. Thurs. Fri. Sat.

Individual goal (lengths of meditation): ____________

Gratitude journal

Two small things:

Two bigger things:

Social Connection

Mark each day of the week you talked or smiled at a stranger or talked to a friend.

Sun. Mon. Tues. Wed. Thurs. Fri. Sat.

This week I feel:

This week I will focus on:

Circle one or two:

Sleep	Gratitude	Exercise
Meditation	Kindness	Connection

Sleep

Mark each day of the week you got more than 7 hours of sleep.

Sun. Mon. Tues. Wed. Thurs. Fri. Sat.

Acts of Kindness

Choose one day of the week to do five kind things. Research shows highest amount of happiness happens when you do five kind things on one day instead of one kind thing a day.

1. ______
2. ______
3. ______
4. ______
5. ______

Bonus ______

Exercise

Mark each day of the week when you exercised more than 30 minutes.

Sun. Mon. Tues. Wed. Thurs. Fri. Sat.

Type of exercise: ______

Goal: How many days of the week: ______

Week: ____________

Meditation

Mark each day of the week you meditated.

Sun. Mon. Tues. Wed. Thurs. Fri. Sat.

Individual goal (lengths of meditation): __________

Gratitude journal

Two small things:

Two bigger things:

Social Connection

Mark each day of the week you talked or smiled at a stranger or talked to a friend.

Sun. Mon. Tues. Wed. Thurs. Fri. Sat.

This week I feel:

This week I will focus on:

Circle one or two:

Sleep	Gratitude	Exercise
Meditation	Kindness	Connection

Sleep

Mark each day of the week you got more than 7 hours of sleep.

Sun. Mon. Tues. Wed. Thurs. Fri. Sat.

Acts of Kindness

Choose one day of the week to do five kind things. Research shows highest amount of happiness happens when you do five kind things on one day instead of one kind thing a day.

1. ______
2. ______
3. ______
4. ______
5. ______

Bonus ______

Exercise

Mark each day of the week when you exercised more than 30 minutes.

Sun. Mon. Tues. Wed. Thurs. Fri. Sat.

Type of exercise: ______

Goal: How many days of the week: ______

Week: ______________

Meditation

Mark each day of the week you meditated.

Sun. Mon. Tues. Wed. Thurs. Fri. Sat.

Individual goal (lengths of meditation): ______________

Gratitude journal

Two small things:

____

____

____

____

Two bigger things:

____

____

____

____

Social Connection

Mark each day of the week you talked or smiled at a stranger or talked to a friend.

Sun. Mon. Tues. Wed. Thurs. Fri. Sat.

This week I feel:

This week I will focus on:

Circle one or two:

Sleep	Gratitude	Exercise
Meditation	Kindness	Connection

Sleep

Mark each day of the week you got more than 7 hours of sleep.

Sun. Mon. Tues. Wed. Thurs. Fri. Sat.

Acts of Kindness

Choose one day of the week to do five kind things. Research shows highest amount of happiness happens when you do five kind things on one day instead of one kind thing a day.

1.
2.
3.
4.
5.

Bonus

Exercise

Mark each day of the week when you exercised more than 30 minutes.

Sun. Mon. Tues. Wed. Thurs. Fri. Sat.

Type of exercise: ____________________

Goal: How many days of the week: __________

Week: ____ ____

Meditation

Mark each day of the week you meditated.

Sun. Mon. Tues. Wed. Thurs. Fri. Sat.

Individual goal (lengths of meditation): ____________

Gratitude journal

Two small things:

____

____

____

____

Two bigger things:

____

____

____

____

Social Connection

Mark each day of the week you talked or smiled at a stranger or talked to a friend.

Sun. Mon. Tues. Wed. Thurs. Fri. Sat.

This week I feel:

This week I will focus on:

Circle one or two:

Sleep	Gratitude	Exercise
Meditation	Kindness	Connection

Sleep

Mark each day of the week you got more than 7 hours of sleep.

Sun. Mon. Tues. Wed. Thurs. Fri. Sat.

Acts of Kindness

Choose one day of the week to do five kind things. Research shows highest amount of happiness happens when you do five kind things on one day instead of one kind thing a day.

1. ______________________________
2. ______________________________
3. ______________________________
4. ______________________________
5. ______________________________

Bonus ______________________________

Exercise

Mark each day of the week when you exercised more than 30 minutes.

Sun. Mon. Tues. Wed. Thurs. Fri. Sat.

Type of exercise: ____________________

Goal: How many days of the week: __________

Week: ____________

Meditation

Mark each day of the week you meditated.

Sun. Mon. Tues. Wed. Thurs. Fri. Sat.

Individual goal (lengths of meditation): ____________

Gratitude journal

Two small things:

Two bigger things:

Social Connection

Mark each day of the week you talked or smiled at a stranger or talked to a friend.

Sun. Mon. Tues. Wed. Thurs. Fri. Sat.

This week I feel:

This week I will focus on:

Circle one or two:

Sleep	Gratitude	Exercise
Meditation	Kindness	Connection

Sleep

Mark each day of the week you got more than 7 hours of sleep.

Sun. Mon. Tues. Wed. Thurs. Fri. Sat.

Acts of Kindness

Choose one day of the week to do five kind things. Research shows highest amount of happiness happens when you do five kind things on one day instead of one kind thing a day.

1. ______
2. ______
3. ______
4. ______
5. ______

Bonus ______

Exercise

Mark each day of the week when you exercised more than 30 minutes.

Sun. Mon. Tues. Wed. Thurs. Fri. Sat.

Type of exercise: ______

Goal: How many days of the week: ______

Week: ____________

Meditation

Mark each day of the week you meditated.

Sun. Mon. Tues. Wed. Thurs. Fri. Sat.

Individual goal (lengths of meditation): ____________

Gratitude journal

Two small things:

____

____

____

____

Two bigger things:

____

____

____

____

Social Connection

Mark each day of the week you talked or smiled at a stranger or talked to a friend.

Sun. Mon. Tues. Wed. Thurs. Fri. Sat.

This week I feel:

This week I will focus on:

Circle one or two:

Sleep	Gratitude	Exercise
Meditation	Kindness	Connection

Sleep

Mark each day of the week you got more than 7 hours of sleep.

Sun. Mon. Tues. Wed. Thurs. Fri. Sat.

Acts of Kindness

Choose one day of the week to do five kind things. Research shows highest amount of happiness happens when you do five kind things on one day instead of one kind thing a day.

1. ______
2. ______
3. ______
4. ______
5. ______

Bonus ______

Exercise

Mark each day of the week when you exercised more than 30 minutes.

Sun. Mon. Tues. Wed. Thurs. Fri. Sat.

Type of exercise: ______

Goal: How many days of the week: ______

Week:____________

Meditation

Mark each day of the week you meditated.

Sun. Mon. Tues. Wed. Thurs. Fri. Sat.

Individual goal (lengths of meditation): ____________

Gratitude journal

Two small things:

____

____

____

____

Two bigger things:

____

____

____

____

Social Connection

Mark each day of the week you talked or smiled at a stranger or talked to a friend.

Sun. Mon. Tues. Wen. Thurs. Fri. Sat.

This week I feel:

This week I will focus on:

Circle one or two:

Sleep	Gratitude	Exercise
Meditation	Kindness	Connection

Sleep

Mark each day of the week you got more than 7 hours of sleep.

Sun. Mon. Tues. Wed. Thurs. Fri. Sat.

Acts of Kindness

Choose one day of the week to do five kind things. Research shows highest amount of happiness happens when you do five kind things on one day instead of one kind thing a day.

1. ____
2. ____
3. ____
4. ____
5. ____

Bonus ____

Exercise

Mark each day of the week when you exercised more than 30 minutes.

Sun. Mon. Tues. Wed. Thurs. Fri. Sat.

Type of exercise: ____

Goal: How many days of the week: ____

Week:____________

Meditation

Mark each day of the week you meditated.

Sun. Mon. Tues. Wed. Thurs. Fri. Sat.

Individual goal (lengths of meditation): ____________

Gratitude journal

Two small things:

____

____

____

____

Two bigger things:

____

____

____

____

Social Connection

Mark each day of the week you talked or smiled at a stranger or talked to a friend.

Sun. Mon. Tues. Wed. Thurs. Fri. Sat.

This week I feel:

This week I will focus on:

Circle one or two:

Sleep	Gratitude	Exercise
Meditation	Kindness	Connection

Sleep

Mark each day of the week you got more than 7 hours of sleep.

Sun. Mon. Tues. Wed. Thurs. Fri. Sat.

Acts of Kindness

Choose one day of the week to do five kind things. Research shows highest amount of happiness happens when you do five kind things on one day instead of one kind thing a day.

1. ____
2. ____
3. ____
4. ____
5. ____

Bonus ____

Exercise

Mark each day of the week when you exercised more than 30 minutes.

Sun. Mon. Tues. Wed. Thurs. Fri. Sat.

Type of exercise: ____

Goal: How many days of the week: ____

Week: _____________

Meditation

Mark each day of the week you meditated.

Sun. Mon. Tues. Wed. Thurs. Fri. Sat.

Individual goal (lengths of meditation): ______________

Gratitude journal

Two small things:

Two bigger things:

Social Connection

Mark each day of the week you talked or smiled at a stranger or talked to a friend.

Sun. Mon. Tues. Wed. Thurs. Fri. Sat.

This week I feel:

This week I will focus on:

Circle one or two:

Sleep	Gratitude	Exercise
Meditation	Kindness	Connection

Sleep

Mark each day of the week you got more than 7 hours of sleep.

Sun. Mon. Tues. Wed. Thurs. Fri. Sat.

Acts of Kindness

Choose one day of the week to do five kind things. Research shows highest amount of happiness happens when you do five kind things on one day instead of one kind thing a day.

1. ____________________
2. ____________________
3. ____________________
4. ____________________
5. ____________________

Bonus ____________________

Exercise

Mark each day of the week when you exercised more than 30 minutes.

Sun. Mon. Tues. Wed. Thurs. Fri. Sat.

Type of exercise: ________________

Goal: How many days of the week: __________

Week:_____________

Meditation

Mark each day of the week you meditated.

Sun. Mon. Tues. Wed. Thurs. Fri. Sat.

Individual goal (lengths of meditation): __________

Gratitude journal

Two small things:

Two bigger things:

Social Connection

Mark each day of the week you talked or smiled at a stranger or talked to a friend.

Sun. Mon. Tues. Wed. Thurs. Fri. Sat.

This week I feel:

This week I will focus on:

Circle one or two:

Sleep	Gratitude	Exercise
Meditation	Kindness	Connection

Sleep

Mark each day of the week you got more than 7 hours of sleep.

Sun. Mon. Tues. Wed. Thurs. Fri. Sat.

Acts of Kindness

Choose one day of the week to do five kind things. Research shows highest amount of happiness happens when you do five kind things on one day instead of one kind thing a day.

1. ______
2. ______
3. ______
4. ______
5. ______

Bonus ______

Exercise

Mark each day of the week when you exercised more than 30 minutes.

Sun. Mon. Tues. Wed. Thurs. Fri. Sat.

Type of exercise: ______

Goal: How many days of the week: ______

Week: ____________

Meditation

Mark each day of the week you meditated.

Sun. Mon. Tues. Wed. Thurs. Fri. Sat.

Individual goal (lengths of meditation): ____________

Gratitude journal

Two small things:

Two bigger things:

Social Connection

Mark each day of the week you talked or smiled at a stranger or talked to a friend.

Sun. Mon. Tues. Wed. Thurs. Fri. Sat.

This week I feel:

This week I will focus on:

Circle one or two:

Sleep	Gratitude	Exercise
Meditation	Kindness	Connection

Sleep

Mark each day of the week you got more than 7 hours of sleep.

Sun. Mon. Tues. Wed. Thurs. Fri. Sat.

Acts of Kindness

Choose one day of the week to do five kind things. Research shows highest amount of happiness happens when you do five kind things on one day instead of one kind thing a day.

1. ______
2. ______
3. ______
4. ______
5. ______

Bonus ______

Exercise

Mark each day of the week when you exercised more than 30 minutes.

Sun. Mon. Tues. Wed. Thurs. Fri. Sat.

Type of exercise: ______

Goal: How many days of the week: ______

Week: ____________

Meditation

Mark each day of the week you meditated.

Sun. Mon. Tues. Wed. Thurs. Fri. Sat.

Individual goal (lengths of meditation): ____________

Gratitude journal

Two small things:

____

____

____

____

Two bigger things:

____

____

____

____

Social Connection

Mark each day of the week you talked or smiled at a stranger or talked to a friend.

Sun. Mon. Tues. Wed. Thurs. Fri. Sat.

This week I feel:

This week I will focus on:

Circle one or two:

Sleep	Gratitude	Exercise
Meditation	Kindness	Connection

Sleep

Mark each day of the week you got more than 7 hours of sleep.

Sun. Mon. Tues. Wed. Thurs. Fri. Sat.

Acts of Kindness

Choose one day of the week to do five kind things. Research shows highest amount of happiness happens when you do five kind things on one day instead of one kind thing a day.

1. ______
2. ______
3. ______
4. ______
5. ______

Bonus ______

Exercise

Mark each day of the week when you exercised more than 30 minutes.

Sun. Mon. Tues. Wed. Thurs. Fri. Sat.

Type of exercise: ______

Goal: How many days of the week: ______

Meditation

Week: _____________

Mark each day of the week you meditated.

Sun. Mon. Tues. Wed. Thurs. Fri. Sat.

Individual goal (lengths of meditation): ____________

Gratitude journal

Two small things:

Two bigger things:

Social Connection

Mark each day of the week you talked or smiled at a stranger or talked to a friend.

Sun. Mon. Tues. Wed. Thurs. Fri. Sat.

This week I feel:

This week I will focus on:

Circle one or two:

Sleep	Gratitude	Exercise
Meditation	Kindness	Connection

Sleep

Mark each day of the week you got more than 7 hours of sleep.

Sun. Mon. Tues. Wed. Thurs. Fri. Sat.

Acts of Kindness

Choose one day of the week to do five kind things. Research shows highest amount of happiness happens when you do five kind things on one day instead of one kind thing a day.

1. ______
2. ______
3. ______
4. ______
5. ______

Bonus ______

Exercise

Mark each day of the week when you exercised more than 30 minutes.

Sun. Mon. Tues. Wed. Thurs. Fri. Sat.

Type of exercise: ______

Goal: How many days of the week: ______

Week: ____________

Meditation

Mark each day of the week you meditated.

Sun. Mon. Tues. Wed. Thurs. Fri. Sat.

Individual goal (lengths of meditation): ____________

Gratitude journal

Two small things:

____

____

____

____

Two bigger things:

____

____

____

____

Social Connection

Mark each day of the week you talked or smiled at a stranger or talked to a friend.

Sun. Mon. Tues. Wed. Thurs. Fri. Sat.

This week I feel:

Evaluation

Evaluation: Sleep

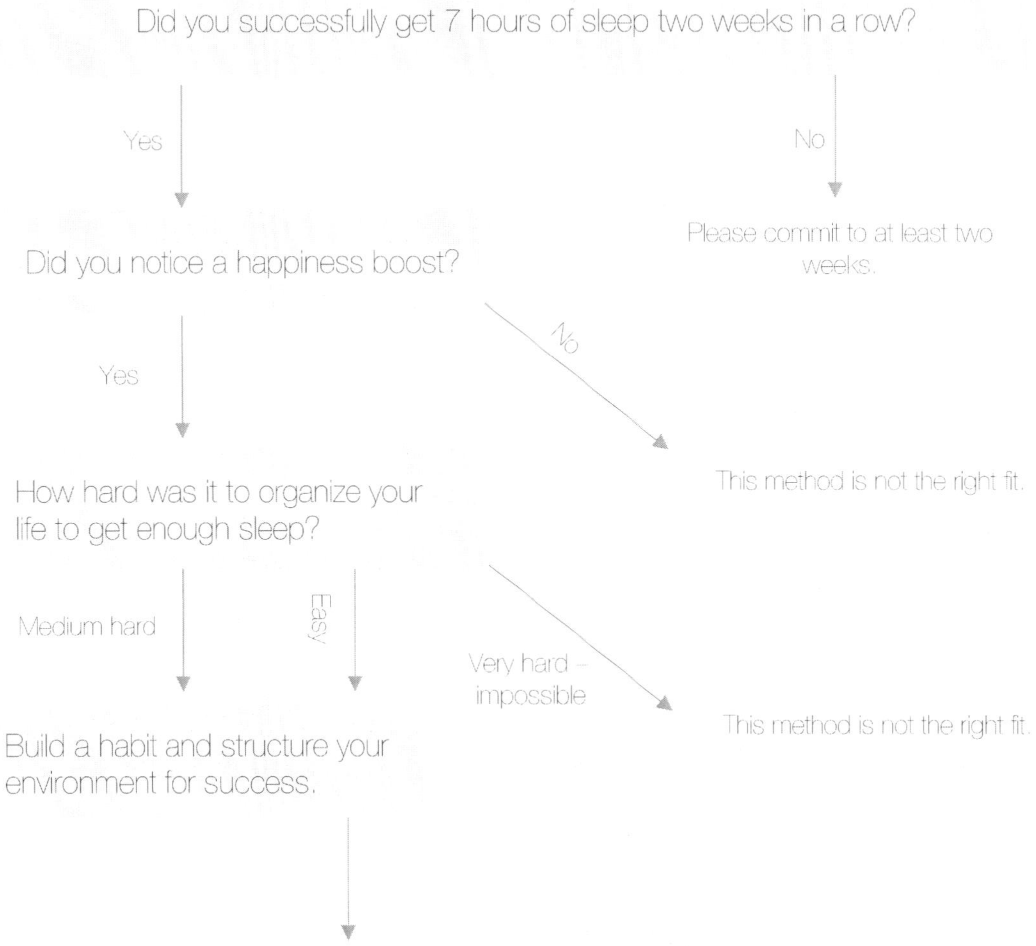

Congratulations!

You found a method that works for you. Getting enough sleep increases your happiness. Stick with getting enough sleep.

Does getting enough sleep work for me? Yes ◯ No ◯

My individual strategies for getting enough sleep

To make sure I benefit from this long-term happiness booster, I will develop a habit of getting enough sleep and setting my environment up for success.

Evaluation: Acts of Kindness

Did you successfully do 5 acts of kindness two weeks in a row?

Yes

Did you notice a happiness boost?

No

Please commit to at least two weeks.

Yes

How hard was it to find ways to implement acts of kindness?

No

This method is not the right fit.

Medium hard

Easy

Build a habit and structure your environment for success.

Very hard – impossible

This method is not the right fit.

Congratulations!

You found a method that works for you. Doing regular acts of kindness increases your happiness. Make a habit of sticking to it.

Does acts of kindness work for me? Yes ◯ No ◯

My individual strategies committing to Acts of Kindness

To make sure I benefit from this long-term happiness booster, I will develop a habit of doing regular acts of kindness and setting my environment up for success.

Evaluation: Exercise

Did you successfully exercise for two weeks in a row?

Yes

No

Did you notice a happiness boost?

Please commit to at least two weeks.

No

Yes

This method is not the right fit.

How hard was it to find ways to exercise regularly?

Medium hard

Easy

Very hard – impossible

This method is not the right fit.

Build a habit and structure your environment for success.

Congratulations!

You found a working method for yourself! Regularly exercising increases your happiness! Make an effort to stick with exercising.

Does exercising work for me?

Yes ◯ No ◯

My individual strategies for committing to exercise

To make sure I can benefit long term from this happiness booster I will develop a habit to exercise regularly and setting my environment up for success.

Evaluation: Meditation

Did you managed to do commit to your meditation goal two weeks in a row?

Yes

No

Please commit to at least two weeks.

Did you notice a happiness boost?

Yes

No

This method is not the right fit.

How hard was it to find ways to meditate regularly?

Medium hard

Easy

Very hard – impossible

This method is not the right fit.

Try to build a habit and structure your environment for success

Congratulations!

You found a working method for yourself! Meditation increases your happiness! Make an effort to stick with exercising.

Does meditation work for me? Yes ○ No ○

My individual strategies for committing to meditation

To make sure I can benefit long term from this happiness booster I will develop a habit to meditate regularly and setting my environment up for success.

Evaluation: Gratitude Journal

Did you managed to do commit to do your gratitude journal two weeks in a row?

Yes → Did you notice a happiness boost?

No → Please commit to at least two weeks.

Did you notice a happiness boost?

Yes → How hard was it to find ways to use the gratitude journal regularly?

No → This method is not the right fit.

How hard was it to find ways to use the gratitude journal regularly?

Medium hard → Build a habit and structure your environment for success.

Easy → Build a habit and structure your environment for success.

Very hard – impossible → This method is not the right fit.

Build a habit and structure your environment for success. → Congratulations!

Congratulations!

You found a method that works for you. Keeping a gratitude journal increases your happiness. Make it a habit to write in it every day.

Does a gratitude journal work for me? Yes ○ No ○

My individual strategies for committing to use my gratitude journal

To make sure I benefit from this long-term happiness booster, I will develop a habit of writing in my gratitude journal and setting my environment up for success.

Evaluation: Social Connection

Did you successfully commit to a social connection for two weeks in a row?

Yes → Did you notice a happiness boost?

No → Please commit to at least two weeks.

Did you notice a happiness boost?

Yes → How hard was it?

No → This method is not the right fit.

How hard was it?

Medium hard → Build a habit and structure your environment for success.

Easy → Build a habit and structure your environment for success.

Very hard – impossible → This method is not the right fit.

Build a habit and structure your environment for success. → Congratulations!

Congratulations!

You found a method that works for you. Connecting socially increases your happiness. Make an effort to stick with it.

Does the social connection method work for me?

Yes ◯ No ◯

My individual strategies for committing to do the social connection method

To make sure I benefit from this long-term happiness booster, I will develop a habit of connecting socially and setting my environment up for success.

These are my personal happiness boosters.

Made in United States
North Haven, CT
05 November 2026

21769086R10061